Aard-vark to Axolotl

KAREN DONOVAN

Aard-vark to Axolotl: prose poems, lyric essays, a postmodern bestiary? Who cares? Some works of literature, through the wonderful and unexpected collision of the imagination and the intellect, end up defying classification and establishing a landscape where many different genres playfully mingle to create a new genre. Karen Donovan's book is one of these collections. Intelligent, witty, and sometimes even lyrically moving, these pieces make us believe the unbelievable, and assure us, as the narrator of this book at one point says, "Whatever happens next is going to be good." Actually, very, very good.

–Peter Johnson, Founder and Editor of *The Prose Poem: An International Journal*

I'll save you some time. Just flip to the "index of proper nouns and terms" in the back of this here book. If you don't want to read about, in alphabetical order, campfires, carbon-12, catastrophe, charades, *The Chicago Manual of Style*, and chicken fingers, then what are you doing with your life? This blurb won't help save you, but *Aard-vark to Axolotl* just might.

–Ander Monson, Editor, *Diagram* and New Michigan Press

Karen Donovan's anti-abecedarian epic, *Aard-Vark to Axolotl*, defamiliarizes definition while it defines it—a hieroglyphic reality, a Rosetta stone of acrobatic apocalyptic ellipses, an asemic semantics. These ancient and illustrious thumbnails strobe, groove out chasms of synaptic leaps. Each entry is an intaglio philatelic cornucopia from a Borgesian post-post office office, staffed by geometrically distorted Bletchley Park code-breakers and die cut Daedalus maze-builders staring at the event horizons of an encyclopedia full of collapsing suns.

–Michael Martone, *Winesburg, Indiana* and *Memoranda*

For lovers of language, dictionaries, and magic, Karen Donovan is a balm to the soul. Her collection, *Aard-vark to Axolotl*, plays off of the images found in her grandfather's 1925 dictionary, and is reminiscent of Charles Simic's *Dime Store Alchemy* and Frances Ponge's *The Nature of Things*. Donovan is at once clever and witty, insightful and surprising, sophisticated and plainspoken. But be forewarned: she is wickedly addictive. Once I picked up this book, I could not put it down.

–Nin Andrews, *Why God Is a Woman*

Karen Donovan's ekphrastic commonplace book is a heartfelt, tricky collection of riffs on illustrations from an antique Webster's. Off these images Donovan bounces nostalgia and science, lust and learning, the domestic and the galactic, and then charts the resulting zigzags in lucid and lyrical near-essays, prose poems, lists, Oulipo games, and very short fictions. With a painter's eye, a comedian's sharp tongue, and a scientist's skepticism, she's rewritten the dictionary. "Words, words were what I needed," she tells us. Little did we know how much we needed hers.

–Josh Russell, *Yellow Jack* and *My Bright Midnight*

This collection reads like a genre of its own encompassing the autobiographical, the speculative, the scientific and the mythological. Spare and astringent in tone and rich in associative intelligence, each of these pieces turns out to be larger on the inside than the space it occupies on the page. There's considerable range here, much compacted surprise and delight, much "power and thrift." You'll encounter mermaids and tequila, pterodactyls and Spirographs, equations and schemata, all in the context of the extraordinary ordinary. "Go to it. The book is open. There will be a test."

–Claire Bateman, *Scape*

Aard-vark
to
Axolotl

pictures from my grandfather's dictionary

KAREN DONOVAN

Etruscan Press

Etruscan Press
Wilkes University
84 West South Street
Wilkes-Barre, PA 18766
(570) 408-4546

www.etruscanpress.org

Published 2018 by Etruscan Press
Printed in the United States of America
Cover design by Laurie Powers
Interior design and typesetting by James Dissette
The text of this book is set in Arno Pro.

First Edition

17 18 19 20 5 4 3 2 1

Library of Congress Cataloguing-in-Publication Data

Names: Donovan, Karen, 1956- author.
Title: Aard-vark to axolotl / Karen Donovan.
Description: First edition. | Wilkes-Barre, PA: Etruscan Press, 2018.
Identifiers: LCCN 2017025499 | ISBN 9780997745566 (6-6)
Classification: LCC PS3554.O554 A6 2018 | DDC 811/.54--dc23
LC record available at https://lccn.loc.gov/2017025499

Please turn to the back of this book for a list of the sustaining funders of Etruscan Press.

This book is printed on recycled, acid-free paper.

For Raymond

Aard-vark to Axolotl

Aard-vark to Axolotl

KAREN DONOVAN

Earth pig

Aard-vark (*Orycteropus capensis*). $(\frac{1}{20})$

At first light: what you are being offered is not made plain. You are going to have to dig. Go to it. The book is open. There will be a test. At your death, which will likely be violent, men will come. They will prise your teeth from your skull and string them as amulets for protection against the evil one.

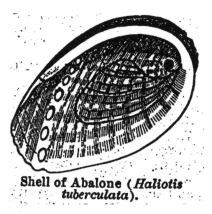

Shell of Abalone (*Haliotis tuberculata*).

A lustrous, pearly interior

Finally, the worst thing that can happen. Language turns hermetic and begins to vanish. Great heraldic sentences unfurl out of the world at me, and I feel no need to take them down. Once I had looked at things with longing to extract meaning and fix it with words. Now I sit on the shell beach, sifting handfuls, with no desire to say anything. Anything is going to be extra. Grackles pick the tideline. When a lady in a sky blue sweater vest walks her two Scotties down to the water so they can bury their noses in seaweed, I see then all the code that is written inside things and know in my heart that words are nothing.

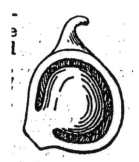

Achene of But-
tercup in verti-
cal section,
showing soli-
tary seed.

The memory fruit

You are not singular. You are not even
really yourself. Something else makes
you: deep snow, grief offered names, love
as portable as a small stone. The time is
simply the time it takes. When she left,
she folded her wasted body through a
crack in space-time and bloomed out on
the other side, pulling the long bright
skein of my brain's neural pathways
with her. A fragrance that can only be
imagined. What I am holding here is just
a receipt.

Do over

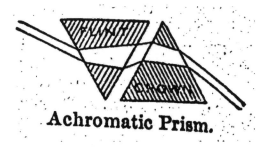

Achromatic Prism.

Hey, you have a very clear aura today, the man said, just before trying to sell me something. But whatever optics had accompanied me up to that point must have darkened remarkably because in the next instant he was stepping back from me and his exclamation, saying, *Sorry I thought you were someone else... um, Janet. Sorry.*

Power & thrift

Acorn (1).

Tumbled in great heaps along roadsides like vast unwritten libraries in miniature. Coiled intelligence packed beneath a smart brown cap. O That Which Has Not Yet Spoken. O Terror of Enormous Redundancies. Roll with me into the grass. There are already too many leaves. The books are full. For god's sake, keep them to yourself.

View from Southwest airliner on final approach to Providence

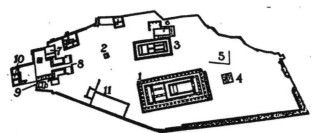

Plan of Acropolis. 1. Parthenon. 2. Statue of Athene Proma-
chos. 3. Old Temple of Athena. 4 Temple of Roma. 5. Great
Altar of Athena. 6. Erechtheum. 7. Pinakotheke. 8. Propylœa.
9. Temple of Niké Apteros. 10. Gate. 11. Chalkotheke (prob-
ably).

1. Three marinas leading in from bay. 2. Brackish spring-fed cove.
3. Large copse of oak and, at center of plan, ancient crabapple tree
bowed arthritically over corner of rooftop. 4. Pocket goldfish pond
containing cold, tea-colored water, autumn leaves, and two or
three fish (probably). 5. Down a flight of stairs, small strip of grass
on which a man and a woman often stand, watching tide creep in
and out over periwinkle-studded mud. 6. Loose boat occasionally
floating by. 7. Bright yellow fire hydrant. 8. Faint markings slightly
visible on street where children once painted a field for four
square. 9. Sparrows in brambles.

b Acrorhagi of *Actinia bermudensis*.

Makeover

Have recently let my hair grow out.
No longer own a comb or brush.
Stopped in at Rite Aid to get one.
Stood bewildered for a while in the
hair technology aisle, examining all
species of equipment now required
for personal grooming: clips, clasps,
bands, nets, extensions, volumizers,
etc. Going for a slightly different look.
Haven't figured it out yet.

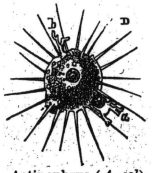

Actinophrys (*A. sol*).
D Radiating Pseudo-
podia ; *ab* Feeding
Pseudopodia. × 200.

Irony & hunger

I get the armor part. You expected
more. Now you can't eat your lunch
without denouncing it. I tried that
once, starving myself in protest as if I
could hold the world to its promises.
Brilliant. An army of one, taking myself
hostage. So you too are part of the
created order. Here's some chocolate.
A little courage now. The world sort of
keeps its promises. You need to keep
yours.

A pterodactyl

Adjutant, 3.

Ice thickens in mud as the tide runs out. *Cold, dark, wet* are best. You like to stand with your feet in the spring with dawn an hour away. No ducks, no swans—it is not their hour. Implacable, inescapable eye. Beak the nightmare of minnows. Your presence instructs eternity. I know you are there, my sentinel, before the clock radio clicks on and floods the world back in. I sleep beneath your gray cloak, which smells of blood and judgment. When I wake, you startle, airborne in a flap. One prehistoric croak, leaving me behind.

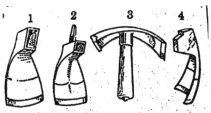

1 Carpenter's Adz with flat head ; 2 Ship carpenter's Adz with spur head ; 3 Cooper's Adz ; 4 Canoe or Spout Adz.

A marriage

There is the tree, lying on its side like a downed mastodon. You can hang your head and cry, or you can put your back to the work. Straddle it.

This wood is green, but a good edge cuts easily. Fear will get you nowhere. Here is a blade that will raise a new roof or mark land with split rails. Here is a blade that will fashion a spar to hold a sail in wind, the wind that will be taking you out of here on the next tide if you're lucky. There is your carved vessel: after the bark is peeled, after the trunk is hollowed. Will it float with both of you in it, with testimonies you have dragged to the dock like cherished luggage and your hearts already like rocks in your chests? Your mind now quieted by sweat, the forest at attention, the ground littered with wood chips like all the thoughts you have discarded but this one.

Engineer

Hero's Æolipile.

As a child, you would observe wind: how it fills a sail, piles waves onto rocks, blows the fragrance of thyme and olive into town from hillsides. You would know what happens when you hang a kettle of water above a log fire lit in a brazier. Make a study of wheels. Do you invent the first bearing, or put to use an idea developed by others? No matter—you pick it up, it's interesting. Now you are in service to love, your days an endless experiment of joy and despair, your nights strung with dreams in which the best solutions vanish at dawn. When it turns out to work, which it will, you'll stand back critically as crowds file past in wonderment and generals and emperors calculate what it can do for them. You are certain of the steps you will take to make it even more beautiful than it already is.

Affronté, 1.

Affronté, 2.

Dinner date

Weighing her comment, he studied the exotic rémoulade set before him on his plate, which previously had made him so happy, and failed to retrieve the evening.

"Constraints are more useful than freedom"

Agamoid Lizard (*Stellio stellio*). (⅓)

What I wrote down when the poet said so. So I had to do everything next on four legs. Legs that were imaginary. Imaginary in the sense of possible but not probable. Probable is what we say when watching snow melt. Melt aristocratically from old shaded high places. *Places where I have traveled, rock fields I have trammeled, being the odd, wise, deliberate trammeler that I am. I am not you. You, who wind more quickly upwards along a marble stair, heedless of the past. Past avarice, past joy, past all tragicomic urges, past available commentary on events unfolded so far.* So far, I have waited too long at this bus station for you to arrive. Arrive, you recalcitrant protestant, at the question of, the matter of, the now what.

Candelabrum

Agave (*A. americana*),
in Flower.

Lighting for your soul in purgatory, for deep nights at the end of the dock, for grave tenders on vacation, for the silencing of aspersions. Discounts for camping without a lantern, for al fresco dinners at the café of nevermind, for attending the flatbed truck parade, for packing a canyon with parabolas. Call for a second lighting tomorrow, for delivery of your complimentary rope ladder, for the flame annuity option, for your name on this grain of pollen. Twelve tapers included.

Fire, Inc.

Agni.

I think it not unreasonable to expect the gods to multitask is what I might have said to him in a hip, acidic tone, had I been either hip or acidic back then. Or been able to retrieve my classical references in the moments before he lit up a second bowl of hash and held it out to me. Smoke hung in the room in a thin line of blue cirrus, as if he were a planet and was making his own atmosphere. Lying on the sofa with a thick red volume of tort law open on his chest, earphones in, an eye on the TV. *Come over here*, he said. A mossy, slightly piney aroma. Words, words were what I needed.

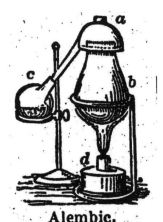

Alembic.
a Head; b Cucur-
bit ; c Receiver ;
d Lamp.

Spirits

Your substance, such as it is, in liquid solution subjected to direct heat sufficient to cause a rolling boil, will begin to come apart into its constituent elements. What is heaviest will settle into layers like tree rings of mud on the floor of a thousand-year flood plain and glue itself to your bones. That afternoon, the lab assistants will have trouble scraping it off the bottom of the glass and will enjoy themselves cursing you for your ponderous carboniferous rationality. What is lightest will fly up, spiraling heavenward as if released from the laws of gravity and cosmological constants, only to instantly bump their heads on the ceiling tiles. Like bees trying to get out of a room by aiming the only way they know how, *up*, they collect there as a golden atmosphere, an exhalation, and when they tire they deliquesce like breath condensing on a mirror, like pale exhaust exiting a warm body on a cold morning. Before long, there's an entire cupful. You do not escape but forget what you were before, which is almost the same thing.

That famous artist

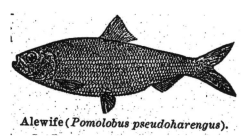

Alewife (*Pomolobus pseudoharengus*).

Come on, his canvases look like they were painted with a fish, she said, aware that the conversations around them had died at exactly the right moment. So she added, *A fat fish that spawns in freshwater and is often mistaken for a herring.*

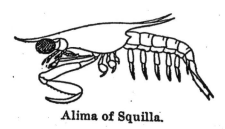

Alima of Squilla.

Proof of concept

Apex of emotion. Bellyful of laughs. Cast of thousands. Depth of field. Evening of scores. First of many. Gallon of milk. Half of yours. Isthmus of Panama. Jar of jam. Knave of hearts. Last of pea-time. Mop of hair. Noblest of causes. Order of Oddfellows. Powers of ten. Quiet of midnight. Roster of players. Show of hands. Terrine of soup. Unraveling of plot. Vagueries of doubt. Worst of intentions. X-axis of space. Yard of beer. Zen of tennis.

Burn notices

Aloe (*Aloe succotrina*).
Entire plant (much reduced). Single flower (⅓).

Until it blistered and peeled, my nose every summer. Driving down a street in Fort Lauderdale, the inside of my right calf on the exhaust pipe of Rocko's motorcycle. With damp matches, in a corner of a parking lot in Springfield, Massachusetts, all of my boyfriend's love letters the morning after he left me. With an unreliable iron, the night before leaving for a job interview in New York, a wedge-shaped scorch on a white blouse. As we drove through and later fell asleep in smoky haze somewhere in a campsite in South Dakota, the blackened prairie on both sides of the highway. Any candle when I got a chance. The towers and, with them, my psyche. My bridges ever since.

The sweater

Alpaca
(Lama huanacos). (¹⁄₂₀)

She gave it to me. Or maybe her mother did. I was 13. Or 14. Evidently I was cold and in the care of a family not my own because the sweater was unlike any I had worn before. The buttons were wooden. The knitting was intricate. I ran my fingers over the nubby knotted cabling and felt myself change into the child of different parents. Outside, a summer rain fell onto the grass in their backyard. Someone put a mug of lemon tea and honey into my hands. The room was full of books and record albums. The warm humming conversation of her older siblings was beyond me. I kept it.

Fashion statement

Yeah, those are mine.

Alternate Leaves.

Yum

a Ambrosia Beetle (*Xyleborus xylographus*); *b, c, d*, its Ambrosia; *e*, Ambrosia of *Xyleborus celsus*. *b, c, d, e* much enlarged.

On page 722 of Encyclopedia Britannica Vol. 1, I learn, the classical writers disagreed about whether ambrosia was food or drink, although it was widely known to be a feature of the gods' dinner menu: "The word *ambrosia* has generally been derived from the Greek for 'not' and 'mortal.' A. W. Verrell, however, denied that there is any clear example in which the Greek word *ambrosios* necessarily means 'immortal,' and explains it as 'fragrant,' a sense which is always suitable. If so, the word may be derived from the Semitic *ambar* (ambergris), to which Eastern nations attributed miraculous properties." I also learn that Ambrosian chant, although not invented by St. Ambrose, was adapted by him as a way to pep up his monks in low moments. But that singing you hear is probably the beetles, boring away in any damn wood they please, so very happy in their work.

Aments, or Catkins. *a* **Stam inate Aments ;** *b* **Pistillate Ament.**

Valentine's Day spell

At the sweet birch down the bike path, just past the old zipper factory. Go there on a cold spring day before these ripen. Leave a round pebble in any suitable spot. Walk home as silently as you are able.

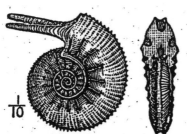

Ammonite (*Cosmoceras jason*), **front and side view.**

Mesozoic

Softness always falls to earth, even when it curls in and turns a key. Ask the experts where my bones lie: there, on the other side of catastrophe.

Unclear on the instructions

Anamorphoscope. *A* Distorted Picture; *B* Mirror, showing Image in Normal Proportions.

On the traffic island at the corner of Thurbers and Eddy, backed up against the stop sign: there was the man with damaged feet who said *God bless* every time you gave him a dollar. Then there was the entrepreneur, hatless and artless in the cold, who strode up and down the line of cars, gesticulating at our rolled-up windows. When the temperature dropped below freezing, the woman in the hooded cape appeared. She stood in the snow, holding up an unreadable appeal scrawled in black marker on cardboard ripped from a box of cereal. The person in the sedan ahead of me handed her a lunch bag. I turned the corner at a green light, wondering, should I give her my boots? Across town, a man blocking the end of the South Main Street exit ramp flapped a white t-shirt that read S-M-I-L-E.

Wood Anemone
(*A. quinquefolia*). (½)

My hymnody

A descant flew up and floated in the rafters long after the last chorister had departed.

Late night with vampires

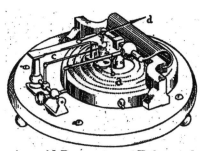

Aneroid Barometer. *a* Exhausted Box connected with Levers *b* and *c* to actuate Pointer (*d*).

The atmosphere was an infected blanket with a burnt metallic, otherworldly smell. Within two hours, we all fell beneath the weight of its profound virulence.

I sat enveloped in the flowered upholstery of your expensive, overstuffed loveseat, wineglass in hand, tortured grin stretched across my face like a martyr on the rack, and felt the fangs of the past, present, and future sink evermore securely into my neck. When the conversation flagged, you zapped it with your cattle-prod wit until our brains went limp. Resistance was useless, escape laughable. But laughter had perished long ago. When you suggested charades, I was grateful because it meant Death was near and all this would soon be over. How wrong, oh how wrong I was.

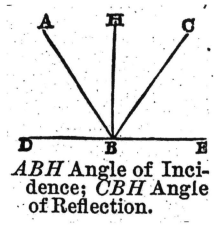

ABH Angle of Incidence; CBH Angle of Reflection.

The geometer measures metanoia

Slammed by a real idea of substantial mass and velocity, your mind does obey the laws of physics. At such a moment, the collision you want is head-on: a clock-cleaning, hundred-percent, guaranteed rethink. Spare yourself the glancing blow that screws you off like an asteroid into space you have to come crawling back through later. No. That best shot. That wake-up, bell-ringing reason to change.

Sales job

Angler (*Lophius piscatorius*).

He had a checklist for how to belong. Know where all the cleaning supplies are kept: check. Be useful in emergencies: check. Make note of anniversaries, especially painful ones: check. Speak up as appropriate. Eat the food. Drink the water. Feel free to have a nice long bath: check. Acknowledge the forms. Affirm the consensus: check. He didn't actually use these words, but it's what his words meant. He might have said something like "This is the way we do things," and what could possibly be wrong with that?

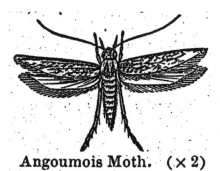

Angoumois Moth. (× 2)

Of note, moth-wise

As far as we can tell, the only thing that Angoumois has ever been famous for.

That fellow feeling

Angwantibo. (⅔)

"No other event has made me so deeply aware of the evanescent actuality in all relationships to other beings, the sublime melancholy of our lot, the fated lapse into It of every single You. For usually a day, albeit brief, separated the morning and evening of the event; but here morning and evening merged cruelly, the bright You appeared and vanished: had the burden of the It-world really been taken from the animal and me for the length of one glance? At least I could still remember it, while the animal had sunk again from its stammering glance into speechless anxiety, almost devoid of memory. How powerful is the continuum of the It-world, and how tender the manifestations of the You!" Martin Buber in *I and Thou*, on looking into, with mutual recognition, the eyes of a house cat.

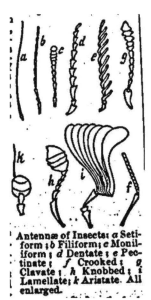

Antennæ of Insects: *a* Seti-
form ; *b* Filiform; *c* Monil-
iform ; *d* Dentate ; *e* Pec-
tinate ;   *f* Crooked ;   *g*
Clavate ; *h* Knobbed ; *i*
Lamellate; *k* Aristate. All
enlarged.

No signal detected

These rabbit ears are from our old TV, the kind that doesn't bring in anything anymore on account of the upgrade to digital. What a racket for the electronics industry that turned out to be. Anyway, we kept the antenna to use when we capitulated to the corporate state and bought a small flat panel. There was a place where we could connect the wire, but nowhere to actually insert the unit into the frame, so we used pushpins stuck into the wall to sort of balance the rabbit ears above the screen. Not that it worked. The TV guy told us the signal was certainly getting messed up by devices in all the boats moored around the corner at Cove Haven Marina, a science observation that frankly we had trouble following. Was the word *corrupted?* Maybe. If I stood in the middle of the room, the image would go all pixelated and collapse. "Move about two feet to the right," my exasperated spouse would shout, and then the game would come in again. But not really. After far too long of this, we finally marched out to Best Buy and purchased a new antenna unit, a sleek little black box with shiny silver dipoles. Like the old rabbit ears, it also doesn't work at all unless it's propped up at exactly the right angle over in the corner of the room on top of the CD player.

Other floral borders I have known

Anthemion from the Erechtheum.

Roses embroidered on scalloped edges of aprons and baby blankets and necklines on ball gowns of debutantes. Daisies tattooed in circlets around ankles of girls running barefoot on beaches. Tulips printed by hand above chair rails in dining rooms by decorators using templates on sale from Home Depot. Sunflowers crayoned in green along bottoms of love notes. Violets painted on lips of teacups saved only for visitors. Lilacs of frost burned onto north windows in bedrooms of invalids. Grape ivy carved in dark granite of gravestones standing silent in snow.

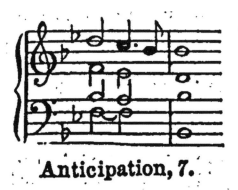

Anticipation, 7.

As in music

In the moment between two moments. First you hear what your poem wants to say, how it is rapidly assembling itself in space and time from every street corner and sand pile and treetop. It is hard to keep up, the poem is talking so fast. Something about blue jay feathers you found in the yard last summer, about the way horseshoe crabs molt their shells under a new moon, about your father, twenty years dead, and that coat of his still hanging in your closet. Outside, in the storm, your landlord has revved up the snowblower. And snow, there is something about snow. Everywhere your poem is making itself, you can feel it inside you like song. It tastes right here like the tip of your pencil. This is the first moment. The second moment is coming, once the inevitable last word surrenders to form and the poem ceases to speak to you and instead begins to speak to everyone else. Between these two moments, the days and weeks and months and years between, is where you live, where your work lies, where you can't make the poem sing, where you must make it sing.

These assumptions

Antler of Red Deer.

That what interests me might also interest you; that something immediate, elaborated and solidified by language, will remain after the steamroller of history has run across it; that the young man lying on his back in the grass of a Wyoming meadow, head propped against a gray, weather-beaten, hollow ribcage of a tree trunk, writing in his notebook, records something exact about the pale sun, the distant plateau, the air moving in and out of his lungs; that whatever comes to us to be named intends to stay.

Sayeth the ant

Ant Lion (*Myrmeleon obsoletus*).
a Imago; *b* Larva; *c* Pit.

The instant I stumble and fall in, I know: in order to grow those lovely, intricately window-paned gossamer wings and that delicately striated, pulsating abdomen, in order to take to the air like a pinpoint of sequined sunlight, you will have to eat me. And so you do. You crack my bones and drink me down. Crouched and starving, buried in boiling sand at the bottom of hell, you are as hungry as you will ever be. Now. Fly free. Get us out of here. *You will hardly know who I am or what I mean, but I shall be good health to you nevertheless.* You take my blessing with you as a warning.

The accident

Aphrodite on the Swan. From a Greek Vase.

The thing is, when I fell off I wasn't actually going that fast. A little too much english on the handlebars, and suddenly I was on the grass with the bike on top of me, a disturbingly loud crunchy sound having come from the vicinity of my right shoulder. I've had spectacular flights from bikes before, particularly one time in grade school when I managed to shave both knees, both elbows, and the bridge of my nose with gravel, but I could tell right away this one was bad. Yeah. Now I ride the stationary bike at the Y, the one that's like a videogame. I pick a route, cycle through the gears, and pedal sweatily while onscreen an endlessly generated environment unscrolls before me in an illusion of depth. The sense that I am traveling. The persuasion of the simulacrum. Perfect rolling hills, perfect forest glades, perfect seascapes and mountainscapes and cityscapes eternally moving past under unchanging, immortal skies.

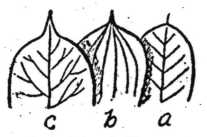

a Apiculate ; *b* Mucronate ;
c Cuspidate.

Also known as leaves

The vernal feathers of my disposition. Flags of many nations. Rain tympani. Pirates of light. Contentious essays submitted for an ungraded course in economics. Some machinery we couldn't invent. Breathers and tremblers. Random tongues for wind. Salad for caterpillars. The soon-to-be-fallen. The soon-to-rise-again.

Apteryx (*A. mantelli*). (⅛)

A fortune

You will not soar. Nor sing melodies from fragrant heights of fir trees, nor cross the vast empty sky with your flock under moonlight. You will not. You will keep your feet on the ground and build the softest, sweetest, safest burrow you can. You will raise your chicks and get your living from paying attention to what is right in front of you. Draw a low profile, pay your accounts, honor the commons. All around you, the strange lands roll out toward far horizons in every compass direction. Resist them. *Fire thou a will. Defeat give scorn. Believe thyself divine.*

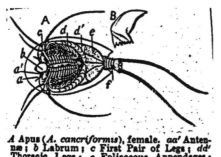

A Apus (*A. cancriformis*), female. *aa'* Antennæ; *b* Labrum; *c* First Pair of Legs; *dd'* Thoracic Legs; *e* Foliaceous Appendages; *f* Abdomen. (⅓) *B* Mandible, enlarged.

Anatomized

She presses her thumbs in. "Your splenius. Your scapulae. Your supraspinatus, infraspinatus. Rhomboid, trapezius, deltoid. Your teres minor, teres major. Latissimus dorsi." So much lovely Latinate. So much bunched-up syntax resolving itself into sentences. Floating here on the massage table in heated flannel sheets, timeless, mindless. Nominative, genitive, vocative. Whatever she wants to call it.

Infrastructure

Roman Aqueduct at Nîmes.

They have bulldozed half the meadow next to Lighthouse
Marina and completely blocked the view of the cove for all
the tiny existing houses on Narragansett Ave in order to erect
nine identical colonials, none of which has yet been sold. Two
of the houses are about half-finished, sitting atop their naked
foundations like teeth on receding gum lines, surrounded by piles
of dirt strewn with stones that have probably lain undisturbed
since the last glaciation. A battered wooden sign on the corner
announces the building partners, the long-past completion date.
I poked around the worksite today, such is my scavenger habit,
looking for discarded but valuable objects. Settled on this chunk
of puddingstone. It has a cleaved edge, as if sawn to fit an old
wall or some other finished surface. It's resting presently at my
right elbow, holding down a note I wrote to myself regarding my
upcoming high school reunion, when and where, RSVP date, etc.
I really have to remember to go to that.

Take the position please

Arabesque.

A decorative style. Yes. Also in ballet. Commands embedded deep in my amygdala issue forth in our teacher's voice. "Weight on front foot, other foot back with pointed toe just touching floor, knee rotated out, one arm extended up at angle, one arm extended down at angle, all angles correct, eye fixed on raised hand. And hold." Even now, fifty years later, if anyone within earshot happens to say this word, it's hard to keep my body from displaying automatic obedience. Okay, I just stood up and did one.

The fan

Arapaima (*Arapaima gigas*). $\frac{1}{96}$

One-ninety-sixth to scale? Whoa. No fooling. You really are *gigas*.
Would you sign my chest with this Sharpie?

Go ahead and shoot

Arbalest.

You are going to miss anyway because of my: (a) indeterminate thermostat, (b) belief in my own invisibility, formed by years of practice underwater, (c) tendency to pay attention to you long before you decide whether you want me to, (d) willingness to consider how this is like that, (e) trickster packrat behavior and prestidigitation with infinite set theory, involving collections of rocks, clamshells, feathers, volunteer pinecones, acorns, seed pods, gnarly twigs, etc., (f) spaceshot preoccupation with punctuating this sentence, (g) heart being already so multiply-pierced you could drive a truck through it, (h) early onset to a default of *as if*, (i) record of victory at dodgeball.

Sam Spade drops the dame

Arbutus (2) (*Epigæa repens*).

So. I did my homework on you, sister. You ain't just a nice flowering shrub of the Mediterranean, western Europe, and North America, aka madrone, aka strawberry tree. Nooo. You are an unincorporated community in the state of Maryland. A record label in Montreal. A sleek bistro in Soho. A software company for, let me see here, audit analytics. Right. A line of fancy quartz watches. And get this: a Google type font. Yeah, that was just the first few hits. I also hear from reliable sources that you have a cheap little thing operating on the side with the Emperor Moth. Aw, cut it, bird. Tears won't work on me anymore. You can turn off the waterworks. Sweetheart, you're going down.

Remains of Archæopteryx.
(× 1/10).

Roadkill

The last one? Actually? Wow. If I had known that, I definitely would not have aimed for it.

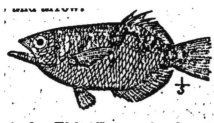

Archer Fish (*Toxotes jaculator*).

Language

It was then I understood I had a razor-tipped device inside me that could spear any prey I desired.

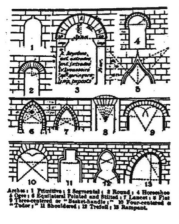

Through this doorway

(1) Great portal of forgetfulness, that history had no beginning. (2) An opening in a hedge where yellowjackets nest and the neighbor's black dog sees me coming. (3) Today's split-second magic spell: may all be well in this dark house. (4) A key in the pocket of my jeans, freedom of never asking the next question. (5) A tower room, a Greek patroness, a lunatic dishwasher, a boyfriend who would not wait. (6) A playhouse on a wooded path headed away from any direction I want to be going, a taste like chemical ambition, uncertain toeholds, too many trains. (7) Last betrayals, head-on impacts, mythic dividings of household goods carried out onto the sidewalk. (8) Peace, art, work, rest. (9) An unoccluded view, snow on city streets, a primer on bees. (10) Walnut trees in every kind of weather. (11) Unexpected terrain of snakes and rainbows eventually domesticated by a rented lawnmower, a retinue of random companions, chimney swifts at dusk, sound of linen thread being pulled through paper. (12) A perch in leafy corridors, all my pasts flying home for accounting. (13) A jar for capturing sunlight bounced off water, a stick fire under a sliver of moon, our bed, sand forever riding in on our shoes.

Namesake

Archimedes
(*A. worthe-
ni*).

Yours was a pretty famous guy. He lived a long time ago in Greece and invented a bunch of useful machines, including a screw that lifts water from a lower to a higher level when you turn it. Very handy. It's an open question whether he got this idea from you. That would have made him an expert on Paleozoic corals in addition to all the other cool shit he was into. I guess we'll never know, since both of you have been extinct for a good long while now.

Curlers

Argali (*Ovis argali*).

Girlhood. There was a home perm incident, but the lack of photographic evidence suggests it did not go well. There were nights of sleeping on rollers tightly wrapped in a kerchief as my hair attempted to dry into shapes it did not comprehend. It refused to do anything except spill out from the top of my head and fall straighter than light into the lowest energy state possible. There was, I regret to report, use of a substance called dippity-do. An effort was made. There were judgments. Then the seventies dawned. Women cleared their beauty shelves with one sweep of an arm, wrote manifestos, and started wearing construction boots. Undergarments burned joyfully in the streets. Everyone gave up on their hair, and I was saved.

Her paper nautilus

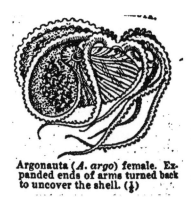

Argonauta (*A. argo*) female. Expanded ends of arms turned back to uncover the shell. (½)

I pull down my copy from the shelf. *A Marianne Moore Reader.* On the cover the poet poses in her tricorn hat and black cape, considering the photographer as if collecting a specimen. I see that I bought this copy used: a price of $3.50 is drawn in soft pencil on the top corner of the half-title page. Blue-eyed, eight-armed, pelagic, the creature carries its eggs in a wafer-thin shell it builds especially for this purpose. A nest that falls away after they hatch, burying form and pattern in the fossil layer. "I feel that I would not be worth a button if not grateful to be preserved from myself, and informed if what I have written is not to the point." When you tell me my problem, finally, is that I have never known where I belong, I think you may be right.

About echinoderms

Aristotle's Lantern.

You think your heart is a pump, but look again. It's really a beach rose in the center of your chest, a curved assassin's knife held at the throat of your beloved, a valley filled with wind. The kind of wind that pine trees breathe or that conveys in the indistinct music of children's voices a narrative of joy and contention. If I could carry a tune in a bucket, it would be that tune. It would sound like orange coals hissing or minnows swimming circles in a little bit of water. They are not the only ones whispering *how did we get here again?* Gather two objects and then see how hard it is to keep them from turning into each other. My bucket would be inside everything—I could pour light into it or out of it. It would be built to contain our perfect living vitals. They will even find it when they first tear the sea urchin apart. Everywhere, even at the bottom of the ocean, a lamp we know we've seen before.

Indelible

Armor showing Ailettes, *A, A* (A. D. 1320).

Both of you in snowsuits, how your arms stuck out from your sides. Like kites about to go airborne, cheeks red with winter, small noses running. That you are now grown women with children of your own I do not deny, but this present reality does not erase the pictures in my head, an involuntary archive of I remember you when, plus a frantic picnic of other imagery that no longer attaches to facts. I am the older sister. I carry you as a history within histories, and as your sole witness I can tell you that your mittens are still dripping.

Armor-piercing Shell. *a* Cap; *b* Chamber for Bursting Charge; *c* Base Plug; *d* Fuse.

Crosshairs

As I sit by your hospital bed, I wonder again as I have wondered before: what will it take to get through to you? Not at the moment, of course, since you are being intentionally sedated by the ICU medical team on the off-chance you might start breathing on your own and they can pull the tube out of your lungs. As your blood pressure plummets and your kidneys shut down, we all wonder what the hell everybody is working so hard for. If you survive this, your umpteenth near-death experience, won't you roll out at the first opportunity and go find another bottle of vodka? We think so. But we don't know for sure. This time could be different. This time is imminent delivery of a package we know is loaded with either hope or despair. Decisions are required, my brother. What we will do if you die. What we will do if you don't.

Arpeggio.

Hungry

I didn't know his name. He was a skinny middle-school kid coming down the lunch line, loading on as much food as his flimsy paper plate would hold. Chicken fingers, fries, lettuce salad. I stood behind the long tables, joking with the staff and putting new batteries in my camera, which I had brought in order to take pictures of the afternoon activities. He stopped at the cookie tray. There was no space left on his plate, and he was thinking hard about what that meant. He ate a few fries quick, as he stood there, to make some room. Then he took a cookie and put it on top of the pile of fries. One of the servers said, "We'll have seconds, it's okay to sit down." But he was leaving nothing to chance. He continued to stand there, eating with one hand and holding his plate with the other. When they called seconds, he took another cookie right away. It went on top of the one that was already on his plate. He now had way too much food to eat in the time left for lunch. A few other kids came up and grabbed a cookie from the tray. He watched them carefully. Then he took two more. Four. Four might be enough.

Bull's-eye

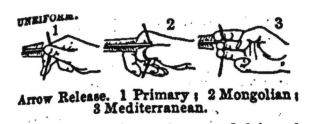

Arrow Release. 1 Primary ; 2 Mongolian ;
3 Mediterranean.

The preacher said that love was more important than skill. That
the world will bow down before technique but never give itself in
answer, never yield a future in return. No, that the new must be
loved into existence. We had just been singing, and now we were
listening, and as he went on I began to argue with him in my head,
wishing his idea to be true, feeling that it must be true, fearing
that it was not true. I measured his words against everything.
My hands hurt, so I must already have been desperate for a long
time. Outside the chapel windows, a Saturday afternoon in May.
Sunlight pressed on each leaf with exactly the right amount of
weight. What else had I expected? My gift? What I thought I was
hanging on to. What was already in flight.

Sea-monkey

Artemia (*A. gracilis*), female, dorsal view. × 4.

I hear the mermaids singing, rolled in their mystic crypts, their dry bones dreaming of salt water and light. They are singing to me, Tom Eliot. When the band strikes up, they answer it, they refute it with no voice. Predicate, not yet hatched, ever-turning toward being, they sleep inside your red rocks, and though the crowd roars and coins are thrown on the floor, they will not say what they mean.

Artemis (or Diana) of Ver-
sailles.

Levi catches a hedgehog

Our path descends through sassafras and oak to a pedestrian way along the river. We descend with it. The Seekonk is wide here, separating all these East Side mansions and tulip trees from Rumford's industrial waterfront on the opposite bank. Your dog pulls us ahead, nosing leaf piles and gutters, recording whatever life form has deposited a remnant of text. Animal vegetable mineral: checkmarks in his index of scent. Never a lack of story. There's a kayak upriver, a little family fishing off the rocks. *I screamed. I was on my phone when he came over the hill with it in his mouth and I just screamed.* Later you will give me a cool sweet drink, and our conversation will be a sort of reckoning with motherhood. Levi stops and looks out over the water. It's not a true river, like the Connecticut, which goes in only one direction. The tide is pushing back in. It will run up as far as it can get before turning around again.

Open a vein

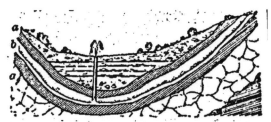

Ideal Section of Artesian Well. *a a* Impermeable Strata; *b* Water-bearing Stratum.

To avoid the possibility of marriage and the probability of long-term commitment, I ran away to poetry after graduating from college. My destination was a writing program set up just south of Syracuse by a cadre of feminists who were busy cutting a new slice on the razor edge of radical. I had a one-way bus ticket, no money to enroll, and a flimsy, farcical notion that if I hung around the perimeter long enough, they would let me in. The fugitive nature of my quest was evident to all. I applied to the local innkeeper, who was so seized by pity and kindness that she bought me a haircut and hired me on as kitchen and waitstaff help. The cook, a formidable Humvee of a woman named Edna, terrorized everyone who worked there, but she liked me. I was a pathetic impressionable stray and ignorant of every practical art. Edna taught me three things. First, stay busy. Even if you have nothing to do, look busy. Refill the saltshakers, wipe down the ketchup bottle caps, keep the ice fresh. Second, use both hands when you are retrieving her beautiful tomato aspic jelly mold from the cooler, lest you drop it face down onto the filthy cement floor. When this happens, and it only happens once, own up to it right away. Third, when she sits down for a cup of coffee after the lunch rush and starts in with her hard luck, apocalyptic, hell-in-a-handbasket advice to you, untie your apron, stand still, and listen. Because there must be some reason for you to be here in this kitchen listening to Edna's homespun prophetic zeal instead of across town in the writing workshop of your dreams, and all you need is for one person to give you the magic key that will unlock the door to your life as an artist. When she says it, a chill hits me inside. *Whatever's in the well is going to come up in the bucket.* Oh no, I remember thinking.

Thorns

Artichoke (*Cynara scolymus*).
Much reduced.

If you want to see a tall bull thistle in bloom, I can take you right now. It's standing about ten feet in from the edge of the meadow off Allin's Cove, down at the end of Third Street, surrounded by an entourage of weed sycophants and miscellaneous grasses overshadowed by its weird magnetic unapproachable royalty. This is not the kind you can eat. It's okay to confess that you find it irresistible, that it's pulling at you, that you feel a bit like Briar Rose as you put your hand out as if. The iron in your blood is already jumping. Go on. Touch it.

The pedicure

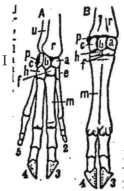

Bones of Feet of Artio-
dactyla.
A Fore foot of pig.
B Fore foot of ox.
r Radius; *u* Ulna;
a Scaphoid; *b* Semi-
lunar; *c* Cuneiform;
e Trapezoid; *f* Mag-
num; *h* Unciform;
p Pisiform; *m* Meta-
carpus; 2, 3, 4, 5,
second to fifth toes.

I have no nails on my small toes, I confess to my niece Samantha. It does not deter her. *I can just paint the stubs.* She and her cousin Julia have turned my sister's living room into a spa. Laid out on the couch across from the windows, my nephew Alex relaxes with two cucumber slices pinned like green coins over his eyelids. It is New Year's Day circa 2009. He may be eight. They are not yet twelve. They invite me to the corner chair and serve me a cup of tea. Julia brings a basin of warm water. *First your feet go in here.* I soak. In the kitchen my sister talks softly on the phone, honoring their business zone. Morning sun bounces off piles of fresh snow. Now they are kneeling down and drawing my feet out and drying them with a clean towel. Now they are inserting toe dividers. When I protest that it tickles, Sam gives up a small private smile. *It's normal,* answers Julia, with an air of such competence that I am ashamed to take this ceremony so lightly. Sam holds up the polish. We decide on purple. There is a farewell cupcake. Then a day filled with forgettable errands. At bedtime I slide into my sheets aware of color in a place where there usually isn't. Every breath of hope required to keep the whole human project afloat.

62

I want a flagon

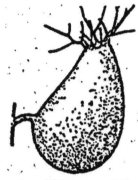

Ascidium of Utricularia. Enlarged.

Of ale for an exiled anglophile. Of lemonade for lackluster hearts. Of chocolate milk with a paper straw in it. Of rainwater distilled through pine needles and still tasting of the bitter faultless sky it fell from. Of dandelion wine on the beach and another chance with the boy I nearly kissed. Of tequila, sure, but forgetting that one particular night. Of blood squeezed from a sponge dragged down the floor of an abattoir. Of nectar saved for a weekend at the hummingbird convention. Of tears wept by every sentient creature on earth, served neat with a twist. The perfect container, if that is possible. Portable as a jelly jar containing morning light. Plus music, mercy, joy, regret, love.

Repentance

Ash (*Fraxinus lanceolata*).
Leaf and Fruit.

One day, after a fearsome battle, the king sent his knights away and fell asleep on the riverbank. His head upon a pillow of moss, he dreamed of a kingdom hidden inside this one, a world aflame but not consumed, skyborne yet bound to earth. He had never heard birdsong so sweet. He set down his shield and a sapling sprang up. He unstrapped his sword and it dissolved into a cloud of butterflies. Because this is a medieval story, in the distance a maiden came riding a black colt. Her robes were golden. The colt's mane was blood red. An oracle sounded from within his own head: *Because we know we are not alone.* He woke to darkness and walked through the forest, following campfires all the way home, thinking, Whatever happens next is going to be good.

Aspergillum.
[NL. See ASPERGILLUM.]

Absolution

Wait until rain stops.
Go out directly and walk
around until you find
ideal leafy tree. Stand
underneath. Reach up and
take hold of lowest branch.
Shake. Repeat as needed.

Note to the goddess

Astarte (*A. undata*), New England coast. Nat. size.

I wish to be interred with these, sorted by hand from the beach wrack at the end of Annawamscutt Road. You know the place. It's where they run into the bay on New Year's Day, the youngsters and oldsters in their astonished Speedos and party hats, crunching down to the frigid water through salted ice and heaps of shells piled on the tideline like bones. The faster my body loses calcium, the more of them I pick up: the commonest of slipper shells, the eastern white, the scallop, oyster drills, jingles, chunks of blue wampum that would have pleased a Wampanoag craftsman. Cream colored, sun bleached, glassine, spotted, speckled, striped, studded with turrets, ridges, whorls, and hollows. The spectacular exoskeletons of the unsurpassed gastropod. Bury them with me. They were smarter than us, figuring out how to stash a soft body inside a hard house. Or if the earth has no more room, return me to air by fire. Mix my ashes with their ashes. Understand me here.

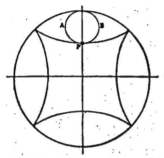

Astroid. *P* **Generating point of circle** *A B*, **which revolves within the large circle.**

Monad and pleroma

For the purpose of discussion and a somewhat palatable geometry that can be sketched on this napkin, assume a circular boundary line. The line divides what is fenced in from what is fenced out, except that nothing can be fenced out but the great silence. Along the boundary, the single point from which it emanates is the source of space, time, matter, relation, being—even nonbeing, which is awarded a tiny attached garage. Also, everything is as full as possible but invisible. There is another point. It's on the small circle. As the small circle rolls along on the inside of the boundary line, the point traces a hypocycloid with four cusps. For this effect, an equation can be written. Remember the spirograph kit your parents got you when you were ten years old? Change the diameter of the small circle and draw another pattern on the paper. You don't have to believe everything the gnostics believed. Keep going. Try a different color of ink.

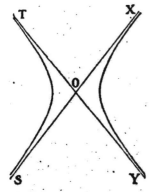

SOX, TOY, Asymptotes to the Hyperbola.

Triple word score

TOX, SOY. Asymmetries to the Hypotenuse. Checkmate. Hah.

Part of a dialogue

Atlantes.

"An excellent answer, by the dog, Hippias; and such a one as cannot fail of being applauded. Shall I then, in answering thus, have answered the question asked me? and that so well as to not be refuted?" *[Text apparently intended to accompany* this image discovered nearly by accident on page 153 of "Plato: On the Beautiful," from Readings in Philosophy, *Randall, Buchler &* Shirk, eds., Barnes & Noble, New York, 1950, reprinted 1961, a book previously owned by Patricia Flood, signed and dated 10-20-62 and purchased, as she notes, at Scrantom's in Rochester. Original price $1.95. Repurchased by me, significantly later, probably at a tag sale, who knows where, perhaps from Patricia herself, fifteen cents.]

Another awkward moment

Great Auk.

Not sure you have worn the right clothes to this event? Resort to standing in doorways to avoid conversations that dead-end at ghastly silence? Blown out by artificial chitchat? Our strategies work for even the most phobic of introverts. Believe in this: you'll never find yourself out in the backyard, alone in the dark, again. Even if it's better to watch the party from here. Tell us about yourself. You there—that's right. You go first.

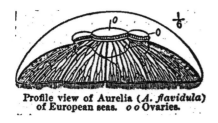

Profile view of Aurelia (*A. flavidula*) of European seas. *o o* Ovaries.

A terrorist

I believe it was banana cream. "Hold the pie like this. Walk straight toward him without hesitating and push it into his face. You don't actually throw a pie, despite what everyone says." Thus instructed my father, the epic jokester. He knew how to handle the materiel. But his friend Paul Solomon was going to see him coming a mile away. A recruit was needed, and there I stood, nearly sixteen, good girl with yippie tendencies. A promising weapons-delivery system. That summer I had not figured out French kissing. I was in the chorus line of *Hello, Dolly!* I was wearing ribbons down my back. It worked. I took aim. I was deadly.

Authentic

Australian Sassafras (*Doryphora sassafras*).
A Flower (nat. size) ; *B* Leaf (⅓).

Although he resisted categorization, we did the best we could to find him a place. He did not compare well. In fact, he did not compare at all. He did not seem to want to be claimed. We did not know why that was. Some said his presentation of self was too subtle, that his guileless manner threw us off so much that we read it as art. Some said he was too flamboyantly himself, that a little less insistence might have served him better. In the end, he had to be made to fit. The time had come to move on. After that, whenever we saw him, the poor quality of our work was increasingly obvious. It was infuriating. We blamed him for not cooperating. He was ersatz, pure fakery. It was our own fault, our own lack of imagination that we could not see him for what he was, rather than for how well he resembled what we already knew. But that only made us angrier.

Harmonic

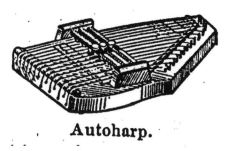

Autoharp.

She painted clouds, he hunted amber. She counted eggs, he angled rainward. She stitched in linen, he fashioned rafters. She gazed at kites, he staked up asters. She buried coins, he windowed water. She spoke in rhymes, he yearned to wander.

Long division

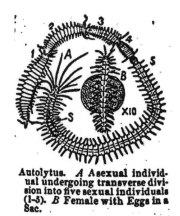

Autolytus. *A* Asexual individ-
ual undergoing transverse divi-
sion into five sexual individuals
(1–5). *B* Female with Eggs in a
Sac.

I am thinking of a sum. First divide by the words *aesthetic concrete*, which were painted on the side of a van that passed me on the Washington Bridge on my way into Providence last week. Take what's left and divide by the green sneakers a friend of mine wore all through high school. Then divide by his orange VW bug. Now divide by the hidden yet manifest nature of the divine. What you have left will be divisible evenly by six goldfinches perched at the thistle feeder plus those two Saint Bernard puppies waiting in the next car at Dunkin Donuts on Saturday before we left for the softball tournament. There should be no remainder.

Do the kitchen math

Avocado, showing Flowering Branch and Section of Fruit.

According to these chemists, you don't have to count atoms. The number you want is all based on this concept of the guacamole. Once you get it you're golden, and you can spoon out your ingredients in the right proportions. Like how many marbles are in 12 grams of carbon-12 = 6.02 times ten to the 23rd power. No worries. That's the avocado number. It's a lot of marbles, but don't be thinking: marbles. Be thinking: guacamoles. Like instead of thinking: eggs. Be thinking: dozens. Instead of thinking: apples. Be thinking: bushels. Instead of thinking: trees. Be thinking: —. Come on people, you know this one.

European Avocet (*Recurvirostra avocetta.* (⅟₃))

My career footwear

Editorial Assistant. First title since Lifeguard and Waitstaff. Midtown Manhattan. Book publishing. Someone had judged my philosophy major suitable preparation for work. Never mind that I'd been hired to answer the phone after showing up for my interview soaking wet (note to self: it rains in NYC: just buy a damn umbrella). After mastering the switchboard, I learned how to use the Selectric by typing the phone book over and over. Getting there was a two-hour commute on the Long Island Railroad (7:11 a.m. from St. James). Getting home every night involved two hours on the bar car, nursing a dollar beer. But in three months I jumped from customer service over to the book side and spent that whole ride home gleefully practicing how to make the perfect *Chicago Manual of Style* delete mark. Still, there were issues. From the ankles up, you look fine, an editor once told me.

A gothic tale

The knob at the back of his neck didn't hurt at all, so he didn't mention it to anyone at first. Excepting a slight wince when what was developing there broke the skin, he was pain free, but we were close to panic. We drew near, but his body was so hot we had to take turns holding him. It seemed that the growth exuded a natural opiate, because even when he lost all movement in his limbs, even when the prognosis was clear, he remained upbeat. Toward the end we had trouble understanding his speech, an unearthly mixture of humming and growling. *Shhhh, I'm growing my wings*, he might have been saying. But that is not what happened.

Aweto.

Axolotl (⅓).

The poet

Every time you look, your friends' bodies have changed, hair sprouting in the usual spots, voices deepening, breasts popping out of nowhere. Soon they will all crawl out of the water and leave you behind. For high finance, engineering, law. For houses in suburbs, and children with braces, and commitments and engagements and mojitos with neighbors. Meanwhile, you stay in the pond, working on how to accept your gills, your strange ability to regenerate anything at all, even a new brain if you want one. Will you ever grow up? No. Scientists call what you have *neoteny*, if that makes you feel any better. It's quiet here, though. Spears of sunlight pierce the surface and speckle the sandy bottom. "The imagination is the liberty of the mind," wrote the bard of Hartford, as if to remind you why you were born.

Night cryers

Aye-aye ($\frac{1}{4}$).

Most of them were identifiable. For a whole summer, a half-hour after we settled into our chairs at the fire, a screech owl began to purr. One evening he flew soundlessly by to investigate us and perched not fifteen feet away on the seawall piling. Later, a barking owl woke me from a dream about my father. Unearthly anguished call of a fox, murderous scream of raccoons in combat, single perturbed croak of a night heron interrupted in his fishing. The yipping of coyotes at a distance. I stir the last of the coals, burned down to glowing embers. The tide is up, and with no moon the sky is dark enough to see Cygnus stretching its wings over our roof. Across the lagoon, beyond the wall of trees, a slight titter. A pair of eyes shine back my flashlight. I think it's time to go in.

Index of Figures

Amphibians

Art & Architecture

Birds

Chemistry

Creatures, other small

Crustaceans

Fashion

Fish

Tools

Carpenter's Adz with flat head, etc. 10

Aneroid Barometer. 27

Aspergillum. 65

Trees

Acorn. 5

Aments, or Catkins. 23

Arbutus (2) *(Epigaea repens)*. 45

Ash *(Fraxinus lanceolata)*. 64

Australian Sassafras *(Doryphora sassafras)*. 72

Avocado, showing Flower Branch and Section of Fruit. 75

Weapons

Arbalest. 44

Armor-piercing Shell. 54

Arrow Release. 56

Index of proper nouns and other terms

Acknowledgments

I am grateful to the editors of these journals for publishing many of the pieces in this book: *Atticus, Conduit, Diagram, Five Points, Journal of Compressed Creative Arts, Moon City Review, Sweet, Smokelong Quarterly, The Cleaver,* and *Web Conjunctions.*

The quoted text on page 31 is borrowed from the translation by Walter Kaufmann. The italicized text on page 36 is borrowed from Walt Whitman.

I especially wish to thank and acknowledge Merriam-Webster, Inc., for kind permission to use the illustrations. All the images in *Aard-vark to Axolotl* are versions of originals that appeared in the 1925 edition of Webster's *New International Dictionary of the English Language,* published in Springfield, Mass., by G. & C. Merriam Company. My copy of this wondrous book, easily five inches thick and currently open to the entry on the West Indian guapena (it's a fish), was originally owned by my grandfather, Raymond Burton.

Illustrations used by permission. From Webster's New International Dictionary of the English Language ©1925 by Merriam-Webster, Inc.

And my enduring thanks to all the dictionary lovers at Etruscan Press. Making this book with you has been a delight.

A NOTE ON THE AUTHOR

Karen Donovan is the author of two collections of poetry, *Fugitive Red* (University of Massachusetts Press), which won the Juniper Prize, and *Your Enzymes Are Calling the Ancients* (Persea Books), which won the Lexi Rudnitsky/Editor's Choice Award. She is co-founder of ¶: *A Magazine of Paragraphs*, a journal of short prose published by Oat City Press from 1985 to 2005.

Books from Etruscan Press

Zarathustra Must Die | Dorian Alexander

The Disappearance of Seth | Kazim Ali

Drift Ice | Jennifer Atkinson

Crow Man | Tom Bailey

Coronology | Claire Bateman

What We Ask of Flesh | Remica L. Bingham

The Greatest Jewish-American Lover in Hungarian History | Michael Blumenthal

No Hurry | Michael Blumenthal

Choir of the Wells | Bruce Bond

Cinder | Bruce Bond

The Other Sky | Bruce Bond and Aron Wiesenfeld

Peal | Bruce Bond

Poems and Their Making: A Conversation | Moderated by Philip Brady

Crave: Sojourn of a Hungry Soul | Laurie Jean Cannady

Toucans in the Arctic | Scott Coffel

Body of a Dancer | Renée E. D'Aoust

Scything Grace | Sean Thomas Dougherty

Areas of Fog | Will Dowd

Surrendering Oz | Bonnie Friedman

Nahoonkara | Peter Grandbois

The Candle: Poems of Our 20th Century Holocausts | William Heyen

The Confessions of Doc Williams & Other Poems | William Heyen

The Football Corporations | William Heyen

A Poetics of Hiroshima | William Heyen

Shoah Train | William Heyen

September 11, 2001: American Writers Respond | Edited by William Heyen

American Anger: An Evidentiary | H. L. Hix

88

As Easy As Lying | H. L. Hix

As Much As, If Not More Than | H. L. Hix

Chromatic | H. L. Hix

First Fire, Then Birds | H. L. Hix

God Bless | H. L. Hix

I'm Here to Learn to Dream in Your Language | H. L. Hix

Incident Light | H. L. Hix

Legible Heavens | H. L. Hix

Lines of Inquiry | H. L. Hix

Rain Inscription | H. L. Hix

Shadows of Houses | H. L. Hix

Wild and Whirling Words: A Poetic Conversation | Moderated by H. L. Hix

All the Difference | Patricia Horvath

Art Into Life | Frederick R. Karl

Free Concert: New and Selected Poems | Milton Kessler

Who's Afraid of Helen of Troy: An Essay on Love | David Lazar

Parallel Lives | Michael Lind

The Burning House | Paul Lisicky

Quick Kills | Lynn Lurie

Synergos | Roberto Manzano

The Gambler's Nephew | Jack Matthews

The Subtle Bodies | James McCorkle

An Archaeology of Yearning | Bruce Mills

Arcadia Road: A Trilogy | Thorpe Moeckel

Venison | Thorpe Moeckel

So Late, So Soon | Carol Moldaw

The Widening | Carol Moldaw

Cannot Stay: Essays on Travel | Kevin Oderman

White Vespa | Kevin Oderman

Mr. Either/Or | Aaron Poochigian

The Dog Looks Happy Upside Down | Meg Pokrass

The Shyster's Daughter | Paula Priamos

Help Wanted: Female | Sara Pritchard

American Amnesiac | Diane Raptosh

Human Directional | Diane Raptosh

Saint Joe's Passion | J.D. Schraffenberger

Lies Will Take You Somewhere | Sheila Schwartz

Fast Animal | Tim Seibles

One Turn Around the Sun | Tim Seibles

A Heaven Wrought of Iron: Poems From the Odyssey | D. M. Spitzer

American Fugue | Alexis Stamatis

The Casanova Chronicles | Myrna Stone

Luz Bones | Myrna Stone

In the Cemetery of the Orange Trees | Jeff Talarigo

The White Horse: A Colombian Journey | Diane Thiel

The Arsonist's Song Has Nothing to Do With Fire | Allison Titus

The Fugitive Self | John Wheatcroft

YOU. | Joseph P. Wood

Etruscan Press Is Proud of Support Received From

Wilkes University

Youngstown State University

The Raymond John Wean Foundation

The Ohio Arts Council

The Stephen & Jeryl Oristaglio Foundation

The Nathalie & James Andrews Foundation

The National Endowment for the Arts

The Ruth H. Beecher Foundation

The Bates-Manzano Fund

The New Mexico Community Foundation

Founded in 2001 with a generous grant from the Oristaglio Foundation, Etruscan Press is a nonprofit cooperative of poets and writers working to produce and promote books that nurture the dialogue among genres, achieve a distinctive voice, and reshape the literary and cultural histories of which we are a part.

etruscan press
www.etruscanpress.org
Etruscan Press books may be ordered from

Consortium Book Sales and Distribution

800.283.3572

www.cbsd.com

Etruscan Press is a 501(c)(3) nonprofit organization.
Contributions to Etruscan Press are tax deductible
as allowed under applicable law.
For more information, a prospectus,
or to order one of our titles,
contact us at books@etruscanpress.org.